Say You'll Stay

For Lovers of Poetry

Glenn

iUniverse, Inc.
Bloomington

Say You'll Stay
For Lovers of Poetry

iUniverse books may be ordered through booksellers or by contacting:

iUniverse
1663 Liberty Drive
Bloomington, IN 47403
www.iuniverse.com
1-800-Authors (1-800-288-4677)

ISBN: 978-1-4697-4684-5 (sc)
ISBN: 978-1-4697-4686-9 (e)

Library of Congress Control Number: 2012901028

Printed in the United States of America

iUniverse rev. date: 4/25/2012

HER HEART'S IN IRELAND

I hold her in my arm, and it's an easy thing for me
To speak with flippant levity of her land o'er the sea.
She has a house. She lives with me. She bore our only son.
Her body's here, but oh, her heart, a restless beating one.
Around her are the things from home, a linen damask spread,
And she thinks of her Belfast just before she goes to bed.
The Liffie and the Laggan, and don't forget the Lee,
The Albert Clock, the Old Queens Bridge, Look Mountain sweeps to sea.
Familiar sights, familiar sounds that memory makes more dear,
And always just behind that smile, the exile's hidden tear.
Her roots lie in Old Belfast town of Neutonards you know,
But here she lies in Canada, this land of ice and snow.
I'm sure if there was built a bridge across the sea's expanse,
She'd start to walk the whole darn way, if she had but the chance.
So here she lies in Canada while Belfast lights do call,
Oh, sea with your wet barren — *be gone! Be Gone!*
BE GONE!

SHE MADE ROOM FOR ME

She made room for me in her deepest heart,
And it larger grows as each day does pass.
She made room for me, of her life a part.
What a future I have with my fair lass.

She made room for me, soon our life is one,
For we wed shall be, sure, 'tis plain to see.
She made room for me and our world's begun.
All of this because—she made room for me!

MY LOVELY LITTLE ONE

How I love you, little one.
How I want you for my own.
How I wish that we could be,
Ere together all alone.

Summer suns would then be ours.
Winter skies and cold unknown.
Loving, living, we'd embrace;
Loneliness from us then flown.

Soon the time shall pass away,
Waiting, waiting will be gone.
We'll remember yesterday,
In my arms where you belong.

How I love you, little one.
How I want you for my own.
Soon fulfilled the wish that we,
Be together, all alone.

COME MY LOVE

Come, my love, and take my hand,
Grow old along with me.
Let us stand where lovers stand,
Throughout eternity.

Play my heart with love's soft hands,
Make music of the soul,
Chain me tight with love's own bands,
And give me life that's whole.

Come, my love, stand by my side,
As you did yesterday.
You were then my own sweet bride,
Just as you are today.

Time may change and time may go,
But still you do remain
Sweet and young, for this I know,
Your heart remains the same.

Come, my love, and comfort me,
My mind is young and wild.
Aging though this frame may be,
Still lives that loving child.

Love is but made great by time,
For as in age we grow,
Inward beauty more does shine,
And loving eyes still glow.

THANK YOU

How can I thank you, my dear, dear friend,
For all the kindness you have shown?
I stood in darkness with despair all 'round,
How I feared the great unknown.

Then in the dark and large loss I had,
You a light did bring to me.
You eased my pain with your tender ways,
And helped me some sunshine see .

I pray some day that I may return,
By the hand I'll give to you,
As proved to me you are a true friend,
You've changed my gray skies to blue.

GETTING HOME

I can't wait to get home, as I know she'll be there,
With loving, warm arms at the top of the stairs.
She will smile, saying, "Sweetie, and how was your day?"
Then as kisses caress me, my cares wash away.

Now I love how she greets with that smile on her face.
In her arms I'm content. I have found a loving place.
She's the house where my heart this time found a home.
She's the light of my life and the theme of this poem.

EYEBROWS

She did love his eyebrows, as they were not small.

She thought them unique, they did stretch from wall to wall.

She learned about Sampson, in his hair strength didn't lie,

'Twas hair upon brow over each little eye.

The story was told that when shorn he'd be weak,

His eyebrows grew longer to cover each cheek.

Sure 'twas not his arms pulled the temple to ground,

When eyebrows hit pillars, they brought temple down.

And that's why she wed him, her browed man of strength,

They were only just one foot short of arm's length.

The story sounds strange, but it is true.

Just watch out for me as eyebrows come in view.

WILLIAM THE THIRD

There was a man, called Henry by name,
Seven before him, so eighth he became.
Each time that she married, the name was the same.
Henry the eighth was his sole claim to fame.

Just call me William, good old number three,
I am the third one in line, don't you see?
That is the reason I suppose she wed me,
William the third, 'tis as plain as can be.

MY ETERNAL BRIDE

I lie here beside you and dream constantly,
Of all of the sweet things you are unto me.
I dream of them darling asleep or awake,
The love we'll be sharing, of which we partake.
As time passes quickly, our love stronger grows,
My face cannot hide it, with love light it glows.
Those arms that enfold me do make me feel warm
Creating love's strong net, yet soft is its form.
So hold me, my darling, for soon we'll be wed,
Then love's passion flame with our bodies is fed.
I'll stay by you, dearest, so close by your side,
I'll love you forever, my eternal bride.

HELENA SELINA

Helena Selina, so glad you are mine.
I'll love you forever while stars above shine.
And when in the daytime they're hidden from view,
My love will be steadfast as I do love you.

Helena Selina, stay e'er by my side,
The way that you stood when you were my bride.
When I hug you, dearest, the world is so grand.
My arms oft surround you wherever you stand.

Helena Selina, how your name does sing.
I marvel at all of the love that you bring.
So glad that I found you a short time ago.
Helena Selina, I do love you so!

SLEEPING

She was sleeping one evening, I sat by her side
And I saw an angel, my eyes open wide,
For this woman was my ever-young bride.

As I kissed her, she stirred not from deep, restful sleep.
Oh, the joy of that moment in time I did reap.
In mind, I've a memory I always will keep.

Now I count, in my blessings, that evening gone by,
Sure more precious does grow as our time quick does fly.
There's no robber can steal it no matter how sly.

I've wealth in that snippet of life to relive,
Not diamond or gold satisfaction could give,
But that moment grows brighter each day that I live.

Here, my pen does record that short minute of time,
And thank you, my darling—it costs not a dime,
Yet it made, love for you, all the higher to climb.

HAPPY MOTHER'S DAY

I've fond memories that live with me always,
When I think of my childhood and you.
Of parties, when family gathered,
Singing songs that we all loved and knew.
How your violin spoke out its greetings.
How we listened as notes rang so true.
Then we'd join in and sing out the chorus,
To your health and a good Irish do!

EVENTIDE

Beautiful summer sunset, the glowing end of day.

Softly drifting clouds that echo the sun's last ray.

Cool and quiet the evening as darkness tiptoes in.

Stilling the birds and the noises, silencing a day of din.

Quietus the heavens above blending all things to black,

Save for the pinpoint stars spearing their brilliance back.

Landscape that melts as it mellows flows into a nebulous shape,

As night quiets even the breeze smothering them with its cape.

Gently, the world slips to sleeping. Up reaching clouds fade away.

The eyelid of day now reposes. Lost is the sun's golden ray.

A TEDDY RHYME

The teddy bear, he sits each night
And watches over you,
When I'm not there, you'll be all right,
He'll keep you in his view.

When daylight comes, his vigil keeps,
Throughout each live long day.
'Twould seem as though he never sleeps
When I have gone away.

He's like my love that holds you tight,
Protection it does give.
The warmth of you keeps it alight,
Forever it shall live.

If ever you wonder at sometime
If my love still is true,
Just think about this teddy bear,
You'll know that I sure do!

TEARS IN HER EARS

She wept as she lay on her back in bed.

Her eyes she kept wiping. "I'm happy," she said.

The tears kept on flowing as they did before,

She laughed, and she giggled, all this and much more,

She cries when she laughs, so her eyes fill with tears,

While she's lying in bed, she gets tears in her ears.

LONELY TEDDY BEAR

I am a lonely teddy bear.

I want someone who needs my care.

Just hold me when you're feeling oh so sad.

If you would hug me, you would find

That I can give you peace of mind,

Then you'll have smiles, I'll chase away the bad.

So here I sit close by your hand,

I'll give you love at your command,

It will be the best that you have ever had.

Remember when you're feeling blue,

That I sometimes need cuddles too,

Just give a hug, and I will feel so glad.

And when you're far away from me,

Our love still grows as you will see,

Our love lasts longer than a passing fad.

HAPPY BIRTHDAY!

A birthday for all is a good, joyous time,

And celebrate each year we must.

Those years will roll by 'til way past one's prime.

Next ones are perceived with disgust.

From where I do stand, oh my sweet lovely one,

Each passage does make you more dear.

I'll hold and caress you, in private, for fun,

We'll enjoy each passing and cheer—

"DO YOU LOVE ME?"

When she asked, "Do you love me?"
As some women do,
Her husband in deep thought spoke not.
Persistent, "Do you love me?" she said.
"Is it true?"
Again not an answer it brought.

But woman's persistence
Would not let it lie.
She said it once over again,
"I will ask 'Do you love me?'
Until I do die."
"Does answer bring you so much pain?"

Deep in thought, he did linger,
And it was so plain,
Regardless of the answer she'd cry.
So he bypassed her question,
This young man, her swan,
"I feed you," he said, "Don't I?"

A BETTER DAY TOMORROW

When troubles creep upon you,
And your world seems dark and gray,
When that sun don't shine for hours,
'Cause the clouds get in the way,
When the work is pressing heavy,
That's the time to say—

There is a better day tomorrow!

No matter of the darkness,
There is always somewhere light,
For with no moon ashinin',
Sure, the stars do twinkle bright,
And knowing that tomorrow,
May bring the sun in sight—

There is a better day tomorrow!

So when you feel that nothing
Is going right at all,
Your hopes and dreams are shattered,
Your back against the wall,
Think of the one you've helped today,
Your deed has not been small—

You've made a better day tomorrow!

A WEE CUDDLE

"Let's have a wee cuddle." 'Twas last night, she said,
"Let's cuddle a bit 'for we sleep in bed."
We lie holding hands, and we talked of this day,
That quickly had passed with its fun 'long the way.
It's nice to be holding your love by your side,
With her next to you, what a joy is life's ride.
Let's have a wee cuddle each night ere we sleep,
Renewing our love that forever we keep.

DANNY BOY (Third Verse)

He did not come, though time lay on her shoulder.

Her winters came and left, her summers too.

She dearly wished his strong arms they could hold her,

'Til she did fade as does the morning dew,

For he was slain upon the field of honour.

They laid him there by weeping willow tree.

At heaven's door, a smile then came upon her,

And now in peace, she sleeps, because her soul is free.

305 AND THE GRIMSBY SUB

Do you hear the whistle moaning?

Can you hear the units groaning?

As it stumbles over the Grimsby with a load.

With its crew a happy smilin',

Saying that this pike is my lan'.

Three Oh Five's the fastest slow train on the road.

Slow the road beneath us travels,

As a dragging mile unravels,

Grimbsy, just this once we'll softly sneak on by.

But the operator's waiting,

As a father anticipating,

A sadistic gleam of work is in his eye.

Ah, but Beamsville's just before us,

As we sing another chorus,

Jordan, Merriton, and Saint Kitts lie in wait.

For those operators know us,

And they are really going to show us,

Three Oh Five will get you home so nice and late.

There's a greater day tomorrow,

For in spite of all our sorrow,

Three Oh Five will really travel on the road.

And the day that follows after,

Is another one of laughter,

Three Oh Five will come along to bear the load.

WINTER SCENE

The trees stood huddled together in their nakedness, arms and fingers
    uplifted.

    Waiting! Waiting!

Cool was the day, then cold it became,

Sprinkles of rain and snow from the same

Gray overhead where sun hid in shame.

So soft, ah so softly fell the patchwork quilt that trees put on of the new
    cloak.

    Dressing! Dressing!

The corn it was shocked as it stood in shock to see bare trees. It was no joke,

    Dressing! Dressing!

Lo! When 'twas done out came the sun.

Warm it did grow. The cloak it did run.

Left as it were as it had begun.

THUMB

The thumb, that lonesome part of the hand that stands away from the crowd.

The basis of our civilization.

That which moves us one step above an animal.

The thumb gives us the ability to pinch,

Herein lies our modern world.

Without the lowly thumb, try to exist and you debase yourself to the animal level.

For granted we take this stubby chap.

MINER

Into the bowels of earth go gallant men,
Bravely full of fears.
Life made them moles, these stalwarts of dark and damp,
Men of sweat and tears.

Day is as night unto them in earth below,
Black and cold.
Who can see fear in the eyes that know but dark?
Here, young men grow old.

Dust in their fibres, their blood is truly bred,
Father, son et al.
Wives and their widows have born for mine their sons.
Death is bound to call.

Then all do gouge like ants to free mate,
Trapped by earth and rock,
Trapped but not lost for with life and hope you hear —
Knock! My Lord, they knock!

Faint and so feeble, yet strong in hope it comes —
Trailing — trailing — done.
Heart of a man will but pause, then back to the mine.
Back away from sun!

OF JESUS

Sing softly, sweet sister, sing softly to me,
Of a man on the shore of the Galilee Sea.
Speak silent, sure sister, speak silent and still,
Of a man and a cross on Calvary Hill.
'Tis then that I know with a tear in my eye,
That Jesus, our Saviour, was doomed to die.

Breathe, breathless, bold brother, breathe breathless and sigh,
For this man of peace who is now doomed to die.
Be brazen, brave brother, be brazen, sing out,
For this man shall rise to allay all our doubt.
Now the word it was flesh and the flesh came to see,
That by dying, He would make the soul of man free.

Forgive us, fair Father, forgive us, we pray,
For the sin, for the torment we caused You today.
For faithful, fair Father, for faithful and free
To follow His footsteps, like Jesus, let's be.
With Your help and Your hand with a strong guiding will,
We will make not a mockery of Calvary Hill.

THE BUTTERFLY

Here's to that lovely butterfly,
It flits and flutters in the sky.
It is so happy all the live long day.
It slides and glides all through the air,
It never seems to have a care.
It flies so high it chases cares away.

It flutters in the summer sun.
It lives the live long day in fun.
It has no time for work. It's only play.
It ducks and dodges for its fare.
It sips the nectar anywhere.
It flies away each lovely summer day.

It worries not of wintertime,
But sometimes flies to sunny clime.
Throughout its life it does forever play.
So tell me, lovely butterfly,
How I can flit and flutter by
To chase as you those cares of mine away.

Here's to that lovely butterfly,
I watch you soar into the sky,
Your wings forever lifting you away.
It gives the world a cheerful glare
With flashing wings that colour air,
That lifting, soaring, gliding all the day.

ADAM AND EVE

Now Adam took a country walk,
And left his sweet, young bride.
Of this fair place he would take stock,
And see the countryside.

I'll be one hour, not much more,
He said as off he'd gone,
But since past three and darn near four,
With time still wearing on.

At last so late that very night
He did once more appear,
When Eve did see her man in sight,
She said, "Where were you, dear?"

"Did you meet some other lass,
Forgetting of the time,
Which quickly for you both did pass,
'Til reached this hour of nine?"

Then Adam spoke and said, "My dear,
We are the only two.
Were you to travel far or near,
There's only me and you."

"It's silly of me that I know,"
She said with woman's eyes
A wondering, the silent glow,
The smoldering question lies.

She thought he might be telling fibs,
So when in sleep lay Adam,
She gently counted all his ribs —
To see if Adam had 'em.

THAT HOBO SONG

I heard the wind come sailing across the sea,
It moaned unto me softly, "Come follow me."
Be like the gull over ocean glide high and free.
It taunts and it chides come follow me.
Then I was wont to follow for I must roam,
Although my armchair called me, "Come stay at home."
Forget the charming drifter, who, like the foam,
Will soon be gone and leave you, "Come stay home."

I gazed out of my window and saw the hill,
The trees with branches begging, "Come see and thrill."
The hill beyond the next is better still.
My itching foot is restless to see my fill.
I struggle with the comfort of fireside
Those softly glowing embers they beg me bide.
These trees are rooted firmly, they don't roam wide.
Liken yourself unto them, "We beg you bide."

The clouds are floating loosely. The wild birds call.
That river flowing seaward does beckon all.
The wind, that phantom hobo of chartless hall,
Does beg, does plea, does whisper, "Come!" does bawl,
And I resist temptation, oh, Lord, I try,
It haunts me, and it taunts me until die,
Come follow, ever follow. That restless cry.

WHEN

For every laugh, there's a cry.
Each sob, a ray of sun nearby.
Sometimes there is a rainy day
So skies will gleam bright and gay.
Anon it is. I know not why.

MOM AND DAD

A couple young once started out,
Like many others do,
With age and time to test them out
Their love was always true.

On beauty's face a change was made
As wrinkles took their toll.
As handsomeness gave way to age,
Their love came from the soul.

Her hand in his, they battled storm
In sickness and in health,
And when their journey found its end,
They had their sought for wealth.

He took her, with her hand in his,
He lead her to the sun,
To love throughout eternity
When life down here was done.

He'd watched her face with wrinkles fill
'Til death came walking by
He'd gone with her to make a place,
A home, up in the sky.

CONTEMPLATING AGE

Ask anyone how old is old.
Invariably you are told,
"You see that gent more gray than I?
Time breathes on him its heavy sigh.
His passion dimmed his nights grow cold."

But should you ask that elder gent,
Who you were told is all but spent,
He's sure to say with sparkling eye,
He reckons not the time of sigh,
For there are older less content.

These older, should they ever be found,
With life are full in memory bound.
They tell you this and so say I,
"Think not of age, of time's old sigh
You're always young above the ground!"

MY LOVE

Whenever the moon is full, my love,
Whenever night is nigh,
Whenever the day is dead, my fair.
And stars fill out the sky,
Then I with heart, my longing heart,
Reach out to you do I.

With time that fleets away too soon,
I am once more alone,
With trains that take you far away,
Remove you from my home.
All things do pass, all things go by,
So here am I alone.

In memory, I see each eye,
I hold a small face near,
Full round, and brown, they brim with love,
Here lies our future, dear.
I pray thee God, let time pass quick,
To bring to end this year.

I bring an end — I close this year,
Start out anew, my mate.
We take, we build, we love, we are,
Just you and I, 'tis fate.
You know full well and so do I,
We life appreciate.

PLEA

The things I say, the things I do ,

I bring in iniquity,

Then with these clumsy hulking hands

I smash with trouble's sea.

I am a man, or its excuse,

At least I try to be,

So let me love just you alone,

That ne'er I lonely be.

MY DARLING ANGEL

From Erin came a beauty, a beauty sweet and mild.
From Erin came my darling when she was but a child.
    Her eyes were filled with laughter,
    And her lips held on a smile.
    I've loved her ever after,
    My heart she did beguile.

I've longed to go to Ireland, but now I need not go,
My heaven came unto me and set my heart aglow.
    She's luckier than seven,
    She brought me so much joy.
    She's made my world a heaven,
    She stole my heart, my boy.

MY MOM AND DAD

I see my dad with crow's feet
Beside each twinkling eye,
His face is lined with laughter
That never seems to die.
I see my mom with gray hair,
No fairer face behold,
Her smile brings out the sunshine
That drives away the cold.
Though grams and gramps, they now be
And their lives much they've spent,
With work and play they've found the way,
They're happy and content.

DRIVERS

I travel down the broad highway as sane as sane can be,
But all the loonies on the road are what does bother me.
That woman, bless her lovin' soul, "If you can't drive, just park!"
I holler safe inside my car and that's the way I bark.
"That idiot. What's all the rush? Is speed his middle name?"
He rushes to the red, red light to play the waiting game.
Now she must put her lipstick on, and drive the car to boot.
He's talking on the telephone. Now isn't that a hoot?
I'm gawking at those idiots, and then it dawns on me—
There's only one that I must watch, and that is plain to see,
The driver behind the driver ahead—my God! That one is me!

HOW NOT TO WORRY

Don't worry over all the things that might go wrong today,

Just live each moment as it comes, then make each moment gay.

How many times has worry wrought a wrinkle on your face,

When later in that day you find, your fears were out of place?

Live every day just as it be, live solely for the now.

As troubles come, as well they may, repeat this little vow,

"I'll worry on the morrow for those things of yesterday,

Caused fears of what might happen to put plans of mine astray."

Then on the morrow, you will find the spectre that did taunt,

Has left a void, has flown away, another soul to haunt.

If we could take up that song "Tomorrow I Will Stew,"

How many clouds would blow away to leave the skies e'er blue?

'Tis fine to know, 'tis fine to think of day that's trouble free,

And it's a making all our own, we'll not let worry be.

And so we have these cloudy days with gloominess around.

Those days when not a spark of joy or smile is to be found.

I pray reflect upon your past and learn the lesson there,

Those troubles great don't truly last. They vanish in the air.

Here once again I bring to mind no worry will allay

The thing that's bound to happen although you fret all day.

Repeat the vow in earnestness. Pray follow strong the plan,

And you will be I do declare a better gal or man.

"I'll worry on the morrow for those things of yesterday,

Caused fears of what might happen to put plans of mine astray."

MEMORY

Memory: the comfort of age!

'Tis you who lie twixt a fool and a sage,

A comfort of gladness, of sadness a curse,

A man without memory pray, what could be worse?

Is memory a comfort when it tears the heart?

'Tis curse of sadness when we live apart.

The sunshine that was, with you at his side,

Has vanished from out of his sight.

His days now are tossed on a storm-ridden tide,

For memory has turned out the light.

Like darkness, it holds him, Ye Demon of Night.

His mind knows no comfort; his soul is in flight!

SAY YOU'LL STAY

A day dear, without you, a year has gone by.
A moment's a lifetime of tear and of sigh.
The time tumbles slowly when we are apart,
But when we're together, it's gone ere we start.
My life had no meaning, I had not a goal,
'Til you took my hand dear, to bring out my soul.

You went over the sea love, my heart hid its face
In fear, just to come out in this dismal place.
The key to this dungeon you held in your eyes,
For in them I find love, the bluest of skies.
Then lead me not on sweet, come to me, I pray,
The one thing I must hear, is that you will stay.

SONG OF OUR NORTH

Sing me a song of the north land,
Sing of its lakes cold and clear.
Sing of its highways of rivers.
Sing of the pines I hold dear.

Fresh is the breeze blowing from her.
Pure is the land without man.
Sweet is the cold of her morning,
Lovely when day is at hand.

Sing me a song of an island,
Heavily loaded with pine.
Sing loud and clear, it is my land,
Far into our northern clime.

Strong is the birch and the alder,
Songs Mother Nature will sing.
Here with the cold running water,
Man feels that he is a king.

Seeing the sky that is blue, blue,
Noting the timbers that stand.
Virgin the land lies before you:
You feel that God is at hand.

Sing to me loud, let my heart beat
Praise, for the north's in my bone.
Strong is the north where the air's sweet,
Far in the land of my home.

A ROADMAN'S LIFE

A roadman's life's a cheerful lot.

Here are some things he has got,

He's got sun. He's got rain.

Got no reason to complain.

He's got cold. He's got heat.

In his shoes got stones and feet.

Got dispatchers, whose got lights.

Green and yellow give him rights.

Got a warm and lovely hack,

Sleeps on boards with aching back.

His life is such a happy lot,

He don't miss what he ain't got!

CITY VS. COUNTRY

I pity the kids in the city
With city streets so bare.
I pity the ones in the summer,
Who breathe the car-fumed air.
Poor souls with a heat heavy-laded,
Like dogs they pant in the sun.
They sweat on their stoops of their houses,
With beer they say 'tis fun.

How happy the child in the country,
With trees and grass so fair.
How happy the tads in the summer,
That breathe the summer air.
The pools when the heat starts to press them,
A dip, then a bathe in the sun.
They laugh in the lap of nature.
They live with lives full of fun.

They wait for the coming of winter,
When city streets choke up.
They wait as the folk of the city,
Will drink a bitter cup.
The cold of the year is upon them,
And salt will fill the street.
They slosh through the slush to their houses,
To tramp in on salt-filled feet.

The country will plow making snow banks,
The children will bundle up,
The country will play in the clean snow,
And drink hot tea from a cup.
The sleigh is the king in the winter,
On country lane or street,
And white is the snow in the country,
When e're it touches your feet.

It matters not what is the season,
The city is the same,
It matters not where in the city,
A house is just a name.
In fall, or in spring, or in winter,
All buildings look alike.
There's not much room in the summer,
To ride with ease a bike.

The time of the year of the country,
Each picture's not the same.
The time of a day and the season,
Are more than just a name.
The picture will change in a moment,
As hill and valley you hike.
So free, so much room, and the pleasure,
To see one astride a bike.

BED OF ROSES

Life is said to be a bed of roses,
And true, my love, it is true.
Alike that bed, what's left unsaid I s'pose is—
The thorns do bite. Aye, the thorns.

Never dread what lies ahead, unknown,
Just smell how sweet is its smell.
When you tread over rose strewn bed full blown,
And live, my fair, always live.

DEATH AND ETERNITY

A fond memory's something that never dies,
Never fades or grows old with decay.
But it lives in full view of a person's eyes,
Ever present from day unto day.

Now the Lord calls a soul back home again,
We have sorrow that it has to leave.
Let's not think of the times that it lay in pain.
Do not think there's none of us grieve.

They a legacy left of the joys we shared,
Of a time and a place far away.
In the memory that there was someone cared.
Building dreams that we call on today.

Let's remember them as they pass from sight,
As they slip to eternities rest.
We think on of the joy we once shared in light,
And we know that His call was best.

Those fond memories left will glow bright in sun,
As we polish and use them each day.
We will lose the pain and have left the fun,
That was brightened by their shining way.

Though the body has gone, there is no one can take
From the memories left in their stead,
To make our hearts strong, although they seem to break,
Think of joy that by them love was bred.

A MARRIAGE

A marriage is more than saying, "I do."
And wearing a slim band of gold.
The poet has said makes one out of two,
And warms up your feet when they're cold.

But marriage is laughter, sunshine, and rain,
A testing of both man and wife.
A book that will balance joy off with pain,
With two welded tight for their life.

The joining of souls may be long before
A man of cloth takes your vow.
The building of one, a lifetime and more,
Before both of you it lie now.

For each tear, there's laughter, each sorrow, there's joy,
No longer is there a void room.
For comfort be found when girl and a boy
Will vow to become bride and groom.

Those feet that are cold, the hands that would freeze,
A cold winter bum in your lap,
To snuggle up close, to warm chilly knees,
Ah bachelor, how lonely a chap.

That road often hard is easier took,
With man and a wife side by side.
The smell of a meal that she just did cook.
A kiss from a welcoming bride.

A marriage is this, aye, this then and more,
You work at it and it will be,
That which the poets have said by the score,
A song? Nay, a great symphony.

THE LAST MAID OF THE MIST

The Seneca sent this one last bride,
Lelawala, sweet and fair,
To glorious end, that deadly ride
Manitou was waiting there.

This "Maid of the Mist" all dressed in white,
In birch canoe she went,
The Oniahgahrah held her tight,
As her life was to be spent.

The fair of the tribe, an offering,
As Chief Eagle Eye looked on.
With fruit and flowers braves did bring,
Lelawala floats at dawn.

His daughter was picked for sacrifice,
As each year a maid had been.
None but the best beauty would suffice,
Manitou would have his queen.

But ere she left to ride the falls,
With kindly look she spake,
"Tradition is fine. Be blind not all,
As your life is what you make."

They cut the rope. She drifted away,
On her rushing water ride,
The rapid water near Chippawa
Did lap hungry at her side.

'Twas then that her father, Eagle Eye,
Strove to save his daughter's life.
Too late he did launch. They both would die.
Manitou would have his wife.

No longer a girl is sent to him,
Lelawala was his last.
The Oniahgahrah seems to swim
In the glory of the past.

Now Seneca sent this one last bride,
Lelawala, sweet and fair,
No longer do girls take that ride,
Manitou's still waiting there.

LOVE'S PLEASURE

Allow me one moment of pleasure.
Let me caress soft thy face.
Give me of a joy none can measure,
Secret the time and the place.

A union when two intermingle,
Love is supreme and divine.
The soul of us each start to tingle.
Now we forgot what is time.

How softly with joy you surround me,
Lo, I am yours to command.
Now hark how my heart it will pound me,
Here, oh my love, I do stand.

So slow does our pulse start to quicken.
Faster and strong it will grow.
And now as our breath starts to thicken,
We are alive with a glow.

As higher and higher our senses
Take us with each passion kiss,
When tighter the body, it tenses,
Praying that naught go amiss.

We now have the threshold before us,
Lost in our love, we are blind,
Then here at the peak there's a chorus,
Souls, yours and mine they do bind.

Let me in this moment so tender,
Softly caress thy sweet face,
Tell me, just as I did surrender,
You with yourself kept in pace.

Our talk is of love soft and tender,
Here as I lie at your side.
Next we drift away, drift completely,
Drift off to sleep and subside.

AUTUMN PARTY

The party is nearly over,
Now the costumes most have shed.
Their colours have softly faded,
Turning brown what once was red.
With trees standing almost barren,
As their leaves are crisp and dead.

The hold outs still have their dresses,
While the others stand as nude.
They gaily will flaunt their bright leaves,
In a manner bold and rude.
Those bleak arms of trees are praying
For the winter change of mood.

But winter will hold yet longer,
Like a queen an entrance make,
'Til we have grown sick of autumn,
Of the constant leaves we rake.
The time will be ripe for entrance,
Before she will shed a flake.

So praise to the trees of brightness,
Giving life to barren scene.
To those who will hold their glory
In rebellion of the queen.
With force she'll take them over,
'Til the spring of lovely green.

ASTRAL TRAVEL

And I was playing with the stars.
Shook free from my bond of earth.
An orbit of mine own I took,
To ape the bright moon its berth .

What mortal man did dare aspire?
Had mind of man conceived?
A spinning bird in airless flight,
From earth confines relieved.

And now again I must return,
To walk as a man earth-bound,
But ever will my heart then be,
Where stars run free are found.

WHEREIN MY HEART LIES

I sir am a stranger. I came here alone,
Away from my Ireland to make a new home.
But, sir, though I wander in place sad or gay,
I'll always remember my home far away.
I kissed my dear mother, her hair white as snow.
I said to my father that I had to go.
The ocean was blue, and the sky, it was clear,
Yet bleak was the day that I first landed here.
That picture it haunts me. It pulls at my heart,
That day that the ship did old Erin depart.
My brothers were smiling with tears in each eye.
My sisters stood weeping and waving good-bye.
There, daddy held mummy so tight in his arms,
Oh! Pull not my Erin of wondrous charms.
Pull not gentle green land, though far I may be,
My home is this nation, my heart, lies in thee.

WOMAN NORTH

Oh, that wild and wicked north land,
Where the wind goes howling free.
Where the husky team is master,
'Tis the place I long to be.

Not a place for men who drink fear.
Not the meek but strong must go.
The woman of the north land,
To her arms of ice and snow.

She will take the strength of mighty,
She will rob your poke of gold,
In your veins, she puts a hunger,
To your bones she'll chill you cold.

But to love her once is always,
And though death shall speak your name,
You will give your all unto her,
'Til she stakes her final claim.

You may leave as men have oft done.
You may leave to sunny clime,
But she calls, she calls you ever,
With her strong, compelling chime.

Never woo this maid of north land.
Never seek to know her face.
For a man, though strong of notion,
Signs his death to find her place.

FOR CHRISTMAS

All I want for Christmas?
It's plain as plain can be,
Just you and I together,
With ribbons beneath our tree.

LOVE'S ARMS

Each night before I go to sleep,
I say a little prayer,
That He will keep you safe this night,
While resting peaceful there.
I hold your hand, in slumber rest,
Held warmly at my side,
While both in Morpheus,
In quietness do bide.
Then on the morrow when I wake,
If you be still abed,
I snuggle close beside once more,
"I love you," arms have said.

AT START AND CLOSE "I LOVE YOU!"

I love the way you hold my hand,
As we walk down the street.
I'm proud to say, "This is my wife!"
To everyone we meet.
Without you standing by my side,
My life is incomplete.

And when at night, before we sleep,
To end the passing day,
We take a moment, cuddle tight,
Then without words, we say,
"I love you, dear." "I love you, dear,"
Thus pass this day away.

Now on the morrow, as we wake,
Before we quit our bed,
We turn to snuggle once again,
"I do love you." 'Tis said.
Renewed each day at start and close
The love with which we wed.

NO VICTORY IN WAR

In war, there is no victory.
In war, there is no joy.
In war, there is but empty pain,
When you have lost your boy.

It used to be a while ago,
That women stayed at home,
And prayed their men were safe from harm,
While on that foreign loam.

Now women go to fight a war,
While some men stay behind.
The world in war is upside down.
We all have lost our mind.

If chiefs of countries had to fight,
Sure, wars would never be.
They'd never put their lives on line,
So you and I are free.

Yet bravely talk these stalwart men,
Of how we must endure,
To fight the fight, to win the war,
And keep their freedom sure.

As on and on they all do talk,
No drop of their blood shed,
While others battle filled with fear,
Their brave talk loud is said.

WHEN I AM DEAD

Who shall remember that I was born,
When I am dead and gone?
When all my flesh shall decay from bone,
Ere I am dead for long?
Looking upon my great, grinning jaw,
Grinning at death alone,
Telling no secret of the life I had,
When I was here to roam?

Who can say then of the life I've spent,
Gay or just sadly done.
Heart that was strong, of knowledge known,
Death I had fought, it won.
Smile at this scull as it tells naught.
Death takes the lip of man,
Sealing forever my life's last page
Started when I began.

Grieve with a tear. Try to cry a mite.
Gone to I know not what.
Life is so sweet at its bitterest,
As life's thin strand is cut.
Flesh that will rot and a mind that dies,
Soul, the intangible,
Thoughts all do perish and dreams are dust,
Death, inescapable.

Life is a spark that will burst to flame.
Flame that will burn and die.
Warmth that is here, then it passes, fades,
Gone like that flame am I.
Who can remember that I was born,
Now I am dead and gone?
Lo! All my flesh has decayed from bone—
For I am dead!

DARKNESS TO LIGHT

Unless you've walked that lonesome path,
When your mate left this earth,
You do not know the emptiness,
When this world lost its mirth.

Unless you've walked that hollow road,
When you were left behind,
Where footsteps echo mockingly,
And resound in your mind.

You'll never understand the pain,
The void, the hole so black.
No joy 'til someone holds your hand,
And gives you loving back.

ON PARTING

I reflected on many a moment we had over a hot cup of tea.

Now the picture I bring up to mind held many a smile for me.

I recall at a party one evening of hearing of a Scot's Cheverie.

Here's a poor, wee Scot's lass born in England, while hubby is true Scot's descent.

Now they are Canucks save their barren who's Scots from the time she was lent.

They are heeding the call, "California" to United States they are bent.

All those things that we shared and the talking I press in the pages of my heart,

And I wish that the luck of the Irish be yours as we drift far apart,

I lift up the hot cup in a toast, then Godspeed as this new trip you start.

When you've left, truly left us behind you, pray think of your friends for a while,

Then there be shining broad on your faces that glorious sight called a smile,

For your mind knows a truth, there's no distance when friends your fair thoughts do beguile.

PASSION

Passion moment all aflame,
Sorrow in thought after the game.
Dance and a time to regret,
Revelation a mark one can't forget.
But oh, to say I do love you,
With heart and soul I find it true.

CANADA

Land of trees and rivers.
Land of prairies vast.
Land of rolling hills,
Of future mixed with past.

Soaring mountains climbing,
Ever to the sky,
Tundra marching northward,
Void of human cry.

Sea to sea expanding,
Cities, towns and naught,
Multitude peoples,
Canada is wrought.

British in reservist.
American in gaud.
French in flamboyant flair,
At home upon your sod.

ONLY THE BLIND SEE

Life and emotion intermingle,
Breath and the dead are alive and quick.
Man's restless soul shall begin to tingle.
Man has to die all his life to fulfill.

Search, oh you victim, when soul will torment.
Wander the earth, and the sky, and the sea.
Death at the end, God be praised, will be sent,
Then, only then, shall your soul peaceful be.

Take away love and a life has no meaning.
Mercy is gone, and a man is no more.
Darkness was naught ere a light was beaming,
Man has no life 'til the day that he die.

Sweet is the drink of the free from prison.
Wholesome is life to a man doomed to die.
Lost is emotion to man with life slur.
Lost is the man who has an eye.

CALLED HOME

God called her home. She walked away.
Although she loved, she could not stay,
And thus, she died—the other day.

God needed her, for don't you see,
She watches babes in nursery,
Scared little ones bound heavenly.

Though great the love, my heart does hold,
My arms are empty, oh so cold,
"It soon will heal." I'm often told.

But such abyss I've never known,
This dark despair, with my love flown.
She left but shell, when she went home.

Some day I'll see her, that I know,
When I myself do homeward go.
Then once again my heart will glow.

Until that time, just God knows when,
I'll be down here, to wait and then—
The sun will shine. We're one ag'in!

CADETS

Cadets: That squalling, brawling, yelping band,
    In uniform they came.
That twitching, wiggling, squirming group,
    Supposedly were tame.
The names, the faces change et al,
    Yet all remain the same.

Cadets: That youthful, vibrant, full of life,
    The body of the corp.
That scheming, dreaming, wistfulness,
    That makes it live and more.
They make you cry, they make you laugh,
    'Til eyes and sides are sore.

Cadets: Knot-headed squirrels both boys and girls,
    You drive me up a tree.
Without you, though, I do not know,
    Just what cadets would be.
And when 'tis said and all is done —
    I sorely shall miss thee!

IF YOU DON'T MIND

I've told you that I love you,
In every sort of way.
I hold you in the evening.
Your hand's held every day.

I've kissed you oh so often,
I know where are your lips,
And as I walk behind you,
I gently touch your hips.

When working at the sink now,
I hug you from behind.
All this to say, "I love you!"
That is, if you don't mind.

ANNIVERSARY

One year we've been married since we said, "I do."
Sometimes it's been smooth and sometimes rock-strew,
But through it all darling I still do love you.

The pathway before us may have ups and downs,
Let's pray there'll be smiles that far outweigh the frowns,
We'll make it to fiftieth with diamond crowns.

I'll wish us the best with but one year behind.
We'll hold hands together, if you do not mind.
Our lives will be richer as they're more entwined.

BROKEN PROMISE?

How I miss the sweet lips of my lover,
She did leave when God called her away.
Gone the arms that would reach out to hold me,
And the hugs I received every day.

Those sweet lips and the promise she gave me,
That our love evermore would last,
As we walked hand in hand 'til she left me,
Now the future I have is the past.

I am living with promises broken,
Tender words that we spoke long ago,
'Bout a love everlasting, unending,
I would live next to her as her beau.

Father Time slipped on by. We weren't looking.
Then away stole the days, months, and years,
All the joys we once had are in mem'ry,
With her leaving I've naught but more tears.

Empty heart, empty arms longing for her,
Knowing only in death shall we meet.
In my silence I live with this sorrow,
When I taste, friend death 'twill be sweet.

IT HAPPENED IN CAMP

The meeting was a pleasant one, where friends met happily.
Until the time of going home, then accidentally—
He stepped upon the final step and down went all of he.

Bob picked himself up off the ground, and dusted off the dirt,
He said to Bruce, "I'm quite all right. I don't think that I'm hurt.
The mud can be washed all away with just a little squirt."

Friend Bruce was shook, no doubt of that, but thought Bob was okay.
He had that little limp I saw when he did walk away,
But, I shall see him later on. It's such a lovely day.

When later Bob once more appeared, a crutch on either arm,
Poor Bruce turned white, he felt amiss. Bruce almost bought the farm.
Here was his friend with injured leg, Bruce thought was free from harm.

Bob spoke of lawyer he did know, whose middle name was Sue.

Bruce saw his insurance too small. Now what was he to do?

Then Bob took crutches from his arm and held as one, not two.

He leaned and chattered merrily of aches and suffering.

It dawned on Bruce, he stood quite firm for pain the fall did bring.

Bruce grabbed one crutch and swung at Bob. Through air he made it sing.

Bob ducked and dodged out of harm's way, and beat a fast retreat.

His leg was well. Miraculous! Escaped on rapid feet.

He often spoke of how friend Bruce did cure his leg complete.

The neighbours watched with shock-struck eyes, this scene that seemed
    quite gory.

A man quite well, chased broken leg, the picture was quite sorry,

And that must wait another day, 'cause that's another story.

SUNSHINE AND YOU

I never thought I could love again.
Was sure it did pass me by.
For when she died I found naught but rain,
My eyes, they were never dry.

And then came you with your winsome ways.
You chased all the clouds from sight.
You brought in sun that did fill my days,
Made blue all those skies of night.

Once time drug feet, it would never pass,
Too quick does it pass since you.
Now we grow close with each day, my lass.
I love all those things you do.

FUTURE OF THE MEETING

Her soft lips invited caressing,
As she filled to full empty arms .
To meet her he knew was a blessing,
When held, he did note all her charms.

The fullness of curves that is woman,
The gentle and kind hand is held.
She loves with her heart all that she can,
With warmth just as souls start to meld.

A prize that invites to be taken,
As soon as the right man comes 'long.
The stir of young love does awaken,
When hearts start to sing love's old song.

So new is this moment upon them,
The clock need not mark off the time.
What's found in their arms is a true gem,
While passion and temperature climb.

But passion is slow to arise now,
Not rapid and raw as in past,
For fondness and caring to age bow,
More surely its progress will last.

REFLECTIVE THOUGHTS

She lies there in the quiet bed,
As he lies by her side.
A tender kiss is all it took,
To start doors open wide.

Embraced again, she melted more
With every passion kiss,
And thus she climbed emotion's stair,
To elevated bliss.

She soon surrendered all to love.
Their bodies would be one.
Then from that height she rose yet more,
To orbit stars and sun.

They lie, these two, in quiet rest,
In tender, loving care.
Sapped of the love emotion brings,
A quiet rest they share.

Those heated moments long would live,
In thoughts forever well.
Their minds would ponder evermore,
Where love and passion dwell.

HAPPY BIRTHDAY 1

Birthdays are milestones as you walk through life;

Happily mark them as each year does pass.

Being your husband, I'm proud of my wife.

Ever you'll be my bride, my young lass.

MY WISH

I saw you on our wedding day.
How beautiful you are.
My heart and mind you took away.
You are my wishing star.

Then we were wed, made one of two,
And thus my life began,
For I love you. I do love you!
Your humble servant man.

I hope our path is long in life,
And comfort each may bring.
May it be smooth and free from strife
That our hearts long may sing.

HAPPY BIRTHDAY TWO

One year you got a poem to mark your birthday, dear.

Another one has come your way; may it bring lots of cheer.

We wish you on this special day at least a dozen more,

With health and wealth and happiness to make a dozen score.

CPSIA information can be obtained at www.ICGtesting.com
Printed in the USA
LVOW102317010812

292553LV00001B/32/P